REFLECTIONS ON THE THEATRE

Reflections on the Theatre
And Other Writings

JEAN GENET

Translated by
Richard Seaver

FABER & FABER

This edition first published in 2009
by Faber and Faber Ltd
Bloomsbury House, 74–77 Great Russell Street
London WC1B 3DA

Printed by Books on Demand GmbH, Norderstedt

All rights reserved
Lettres à Roger Blin © 1966 by Editions Gallimard
Letters to Roger Blin © 1969 by Grove Press, Inc.
L'Etrange Mot d' . . . (The strange word *Urb*) © 1967 by Jean Genet
Ce Qui Est Resté d'un Rembrandt (What remained of a
Rembrandt) © 1967 by Jean Genet
English Translation © 1972 by Faber and Faber

The right of Jean Genet to be identified as author and Richard
Seaver to be identified as translator of this work
has been asserted in accordance with Section 77 of the
Copyright, Designs and Patents Act 1988

This book is sold subject to the condition that it shall not, by way of
trade or otherwise, be lent, resold, hired out or otherwise circulated
without the publisher's prior consent in any form of binding or cover other than
that in which it is published and without a similar condition including this
condition being imposed on the subsequent purchaser

A CIP record for this book is available from the British Library

ISBN 978–0–571–25578–8

Contents

Letters to Roger Blin 7

The strange word *Urb...* 61

What remained of a Rembrandt 75

Letters to Roger Blin

In 1966, Genet's most ambitious dramatic work – and in the view of many, his masterpiece – *The Screens*, was staged in Paris by the Jean-Louis Barrault-Madeleine Renaud Company. This epic 62-character play almost defies staging. *The Screens* deals among many other things with the colonial problem, and specifically with the French-Algerian war. The Barrault-Renaud production was directed by Roger Blin, one of Europe's most respected actors and directors, who was the first to stage all of Samuel Beckett's early plays. During the several months of rehearsals which Genet attended, he wrote a series of letters and notes to Roger Blin giving his views on every aspect of the staging of *The Screens*.

My dear Roger,
Not all the living, nor all the dead, nor the generations yet unborn will be able to see *The Screens*. The whole of humanity will be deprived of it: there you have something that comes close to being an absolute. The world has managed to get along without them; it will continue to do so. Political nonchalance will allow a problematical meeting between a few thousand Parisians and the play. In order for this event – the performance or performances – without disturbing the order of the world, to impose thereon a poetic combustion, acting upon a few thousand Parisians, I should like it to be so strong and so dense that it will, by its implications and ramifications, illuminate the world of the dead* – billions of billions – and that of generations yet unborn (but this is less important).

I say this to you because the spectacle, so limited in time and space, seemingly intended for a handful of spectators, will be so serious that it will also be aimed at the dead. No one must be turned away from or deprived of the spectacle: it must be so beautiful that the dead are made beautiful too, and blush because of it. If you stage *The Screens*, you must always work with the notion of a unique spectacle in mind, and carry it as far as you can. Everything should work together to break down whatever separates us from the dead. We must do everything

* Or, more properly, of death.

possible towards creating the feeling that we have worked for them, and that we have succeeded.

Therefore the actors and actresses must be induced to put aside cleverness and to involve the most secret depths of their being; they must be made to accept difficult endeavours, admirable gestures which however have no relation to those they employ in their daily lives. If we maintain that life and the stage are opposites, it is because we strongly suspect that the stage is a site closely akin to death, a place where all liberties are possible. The actors' voices, moreover, will come only from the larynx: this is a difficult music to find. Their make-up will, by transforming them into 'others', enable them to try any and every audacity: as they will be unencumbered by any social responsibility, they will assume another, with respect to another Order.

The costumes will not clothe them; stage costumes are a means of show, in every sense of the term. You understand, therefore, the beauty that must be theirs. Not a beauty of the streets but an essential beauty, the same as with the make-up and the altered voice, so that the actors can throw themselves into the adventure and emerge victorious from it. What we are talking about, therefore, is an accoutrement. I should like the costumes of the three old ladies to be made of verminous and splendid rags. A few details here and there should remind one of Algeria, but the general style will be of great nobility: full, with trains and drapes, even if all this has dust and straw clinging to it. In a nutshell, each costume must be a setting in its own right – against a background of screens – capable of situating the character, but, once again, this sumptuousness must not derive from a worldly beauty, nor even from an imitated or parodied beauty, thanks to the old clothes; Acquart and his wife must be capable of inventing frightful accoutrements, which would seem out of place on the shoulders of the living. Madmen, madwomen, Madwomen, are capable of sewing such costumes. I am sure that the Asylums are full of these ornaments, monuments, difficult to bear. The Mother, Kadidja, Ommu will be sheltered beneath them, and, perhaps, will be slightly corrupted by them. But please, do not tolerate any prettiness. Acquart must almost be threatened. What a sorry lot the ordinary costumes in the theatre! In them, the actors are afraid to try anything, they are condemned to mere pretty movements, either of the thighs, of arched feet, or of arms and torso.

Don't allow an actor to forget himself unless he carries this forgetfulness to the point of pissing squarely in front of the public. You should force them to dream – those who have no lines – to dream about the death of their son or the death of their beloved mother, or they should imagine that a thug is robbing them or that the public sees them naked.

The screens themselves: those that you and Acquart have made are quite beautiful. (I am referring to the way they are constructed and the way they move.)

But the drawings on them? This is going to be very difficult. Here again we must think of the Spectacle. No pseudo-naïve nonsense. The place to look is among the drawings done by madmen. Even among madmen who systematically feign Madness. Go spend a little time out at the Rodez Asylum. Buttonhole a nut, tell him this story about some other nuts, *The Screens*, and have him translate it into drawings. I believe that a sex maniac, who had never seen an orange tree in his life, nor even an orange, could invent a truer orange tree than anyone else. Where will we find him? Hold a competition? But if we *think* very hard about that, chance will work for us.

I come back to the actors' way of walking:

The Mother, with tiny steps, but the way she gestures bespeaks great authority. Then, suddenly, seven-league strides, with her skirt raised in such a way as to show her legs, the veins of which – blue or purple – will be visible.

Kadidja, haughty, her umbrella like a cane.

Ommu, pulling her foot, her paw, from the mire with every step. But the upper part of her body, from the chest up, very straight, her head straight, the flow of words cold and clearly articulated.

For Saïd, you see, the actor must learn to concentrate. One feels that he is not yet completely at ease either in Saïd's body or his manner of gesturing. For a few seconds, he has been known to wander off to Leopardi Square in Verona, or to the rue Saint-Benoit.

Warda presents a rather difficult problem: an extraordinary emptiness has more presence than the most dense fullness.

It's the Sergeant who bothers me: either it's you and your slightly wild and slightly bantering poetry, or it's the young man guided by you. I believe you will know how to turn him into the counterpart, luminous by Western standards, of Saïd; or, if you like, his opposite in all respects. Solar man as opposed to saturnine, even if the solar types give us a pain in the ass – and, in this case, it's we who will give them the pain in the ass. A good-looking wench in uniform.

People say that plays are generally supposed to have a meaning: not this one. It's a celebration whose elements are disparate, it is the celebration of nothing.

Leila I'm not sure about. Perhaps it's because she advances wearing a mask. I leave it to you to work out.

But as for the make-up, you must call upon your dreams, your daydreams, your wildest ravings, and not upon your reason, nor upon your observations unless they are mad and make you see a velvety fleece around the Arabs' eyes. Make-up intrigues me. It must remind one of, must call to mind, Algeria by methods of which the Algerians are unaware: I'm afraid of the henna tint for the Mother's hair. Algerian poverty and misery must have other colours and other materials, which must be discovered. You and Acquart have your work cut out for you. And I'm not making matters any easier.

And what is more, on stage a light so cruel! but that is what is required.

Let me come back to the actors: they are going to turn themselves into animals. We have to help them. With, from time to time, as they are performing, a bit of The Mother, or Ommu, of or Warda, who shows the tip of her ear. The rest of the time, animals. The way I read it – Nebuchadnezzar, grazing in the grass and, for a few minutes, king, and perhaps, a man.

The Mother: don't diminish her natural fury. Don't extinguish her fire, but add acting ability to it.

Kadidja is already the most important lady in the village: her umbrella will be bigger than the others.

Ommu, a full cut above: much higher than the most important lady of the village. Patronness of the revolt. And if the name means anything to you: Nemesis. In any case, supreme in this death which is taking place on earth.

Of course, everything I'm telling you, you already know. All I'm doing is trying to encourage you in your detachment from a theatre which, when it turns its back on middle-class conventions, goes in search of its models: gestures, tone, in the visible life and not in the poetic life, that is, the one we sometimes find near the confines of death. There, faces are no longer ruddy, one no longer has the ability to open doors – or else it is a strange door indeed, opening upon what! In short, you really know what it is I should like to say, without finding the appropriate words.

And the ruin! I almost forgot the ruin! The ruin of the teeth cultivated with Warda's needle, and the total shambles of the play itself. I mean it: when the public leaves the theatre I want it to carry the well-known taste of ashes and an odour of decay in its mouth. And yet I want the play to have the consistency of flint. Don't be afraid to have the actors and actresses transform themselves into jackals, turkeys, etc. – into trees too. I may seem to be uttering asininities, but you know very well what I mean. My play is dirty in that it does not contain the customary social crap, but it must be rinsed again with bluing.

What I also like is that, in order to underscore – or if, you like, lend special emphasis to – the stylisation of the acting and diction, you occasionally find certain postures and tones of voice that are more realistic. It is in this vein that, at the point of the play where Warda is picking her gold teeth, one or two customers are combing their hair with a comb which has a number of teeth missing, their legs bent as though in front of a mirror. Of course all this has to be worked out.

I was a bit worried about the Lieutenant. But perhaps it was because I hadn't known what would suit him, that is, that instead of being a martinet pure and simple he should blow his stack and get into a violent argument either with the men or the Sergeant, or with the Captain, the way they say that the fishmongers of Marseilles blow their stacks, the chest thrust forward. I believe that at a certain point, I can't remember which, he must cease to be Susini and become a poor devil on the verge of losing control of himself.

The drawings. Let me say another word or two about the drawings on the screens: they ought to be eccentric, on a grandiose scale, but without disturbing the public. Where can we find that? When the orange grove is burning the flames must look like the foul flames a sadist would draw if he were asked to paint a burning whorehouse full of naked women.

I don't believe you should anticipate there being any more than four or five performances. Actually, if the actors and actresses delve deeply within themselves, they will not be able to hold out for very long. Or so it seems to me. Any performances beyond the first five will be reflections. In any case, such is my impression. And besides, what does it matter? A single performance properly staged ought to suffice.

We must be careful about the ceiling of the stage. Even if it serves no purpose – adds nothing to the acoustics, for example – white strings must be stretched from the public toward the rear of the stage. Normally, unless there is some kind of ceiling, it's always ugly.

☐ Raise the proscenium arch (is that the proper term for it?), if you can, to the maximum height.

☐ Madani-The Mouth's acting: he is always a trifle emphatic. Madani ought to display a touch of bombast, in the beginning, and the Mouth everyday irritation. But you and Jean-Louis Barrault will easily work out the difference between the tone of the Mouth and that of Si Slimane awake.

☐ I see the dead as being heavily made-up – but with green the dominant colour. White clothing, suggestive of winding sheets. Their diction will be different. It will be louder and closer to everyday language.

☐ The dead soldiers could be wearing fatigues, rather loose fitting, with the wounds painted on with red paint.

☐ I think that a single performance is enough, rather than five. But one polished and perfected over a period of six months.

☐ Have Saïd stop rolling his eyes. And ask the actors, during the performance, not to let themselves slip back into the movements and gestures that are theirs off-stage, or that they resort to in other plays. It is normal for them to try and find the gestures that are suitable both to the character they are playing and to their own personality, and once they have found them let them keep to them. But in general they smugly do whatever strikes their fancy, in order to seem spontaneous!

☐ I think that the living soldiers could wear the uniform of the Conquest (the type worn by the Duke of Aumale) and kick the bucket in the same uniform. The point of this being not to situate too precisely in time a play which is a masquerade.

☐ It is impossible for the glory, solitary and solar, for the virtues of a man or a people to be reduced, first by analysis, to no more than a repository or a receptacle, that which remains of a man or a people when their embellishments have been stripped away, but the shame that remains, after a life of treason, or even after a single act of treason, is surer. Shame is less prone to being shaken than is glory. It will in fact never be shaken; on the contrary, time hardens and, in a way, restores it, luminous, more glorious than glory, inviolate.

A people solely distinguished by periods of glory or men of virtue would be inevitably subject to analysis and reduced to nothing, save a receptacle. The crimes of which a people is ashamed constitute its real history, and the same is true of a man.

LETTERS TO ROGER BLIN

☐ I write that because, if you read it to the actors, they may know what I'm talking about.

☐ What I'm talking about, of course, is theatrical conduct, and I have been at pains to indicate that the stage and life are opposites. My play is not the apologia for treason. It takes place in a realm where morality is replaced by the aesthetics of the stage.

☐ Time. I know nothing very specific about time, but, if I acknowledge the existence and termination of an event, any event whatsoever, it seems to me that the event did not take place in a movement going from the present moment toward the future, but that, on the contrary, the moment which is going to direct the event is no sooner born than the event culminates and flows back at top speed towards its birth, and settles upon itself. The first Frenchmen bombarding Algiers in 1830, if you like, bombarded themselves from Algiers about 1800. Events are thus born, spontaneously, and die at the same instant of the same movement, but die so quickly that their end, turning round, brings them back to a point slightly prior to the noise which marked their birth. They are as hard as pebbles. The French Revolution, in 'my' story, has not yet come full cycle upon itself. The event which extends from 1789 to the present day is therefore somewhat nebulous, but within it the conquest and loss of Algeria is a compact entity.

I haven't the time to go into the matter at greater length in order to make you understand that the dead or dying soldiers in this play must wear the uniform of the Duke of Aumale and the Duke of Bugeaud. The same movement of time which deposits them in Algeria expels them back into the sea. Even if, by their speeches, we understand that they were living in 1958. That is unimportant. They were foolhardy.

These natives of Alsace-Lorraine and convicts disguised as conquerors ought to be wearing really handsome costumes. Think therefore of Zouaves in their braids, of spahis in their black satin capes, their golden sandals, etc. It is without a doubt the most florid Army of the Republic. Each soldier like a gravestone in the Père-Lachaise cemetery. That's the way I see it. No sooner had Dey's fan stopped moving, no sooner had the first shot of the cannon sounded, than 800,000 French settlers in Algeria were already fabricating Tixier-Vignancour.* Everything was very rapid, rapid enough *to bring off an event* which has neither beginning nor end: global.

☐ Warda must be a kind of Empress, shod in half-boots so heavy – of solid gold – that she can no longer bend over. You can carry her as far as is feasible. Make her wear an iron corset. With bolts.

☐ These, my dear Roger, are the only notes I have, which I leave to you to accept or reject. With them, I send my regards.

Jean Genet

* A political leader, head of the extreme right-wing *Alliance republicaine pour les libertés et le progrès.—Tr.*

Daily Notes

Italian-style theatre is not long for this world. I know nothing of its history, how it began nor why it culminated in a kind of well with dress circles, ground-floor boxes, first-tier boxes and top galleries (what names!),* but I feel it dying together with the society which came to see itself mirrored on-stage. This fulfilment corresponded to a fundamental immorality: for the poultry of the top galleries, the 'house' – dress circle, orchestra, boxes – was an initial spectacle, which in essence formed a screen – or a prism – which their gaze had to pass through before perceiving the spectacle on-stage. The top galleries saw and heard, as it were, through the screen made up of the privileged public of the orchestra and box seats.

☐ The spectators in the orchestra and boxes knew they were being looked at – greedily – by the public in the top galleries. Knowing themselves to be an entertainment before the show, they acted as an entertainment must: in order to be seen.

On one side as on the other – I mean upstairs as well as down – the performance on-stage never reached the public in a completely pure state.

* Much of the flavour of the names of various kinds of theatre seats is lost in translation. For example, the ground-floor boxes are called *baignoires* in French, which is also the word for 'bathtub'; the galleries are called *poulaillers*, which also means 'hen house' or 'hen roost'.—*Tr.*

And I am not forgetting the velvet or crystal, or the gold leaf whose purpose is to remind the privileged public that the theatre is their domain, and that the play is demeaned and degraded proportionately as their distance from the main floor and the carpeting increases.

☐ You will perhaps have theatres with ten thousand seats, probably resembling the Greek theatres, in which the public will be discreet and seated at random or according to their individual agility or on-the-spot ruse, not according to their rank or wealth. The play on-stage will address itself, therefore, to what is most naked and pure in the members of the audience. Whether the public's apparel is gaudy or sober, bejewelled or otherwise bedecked, it will in no way affect the integrity of the play being performed on-stage. On the contrary, it would be a good idea if a kind of madness, an effrontery, impelled the public to rig itself out in strange attire when it went to the theatre – providing of course that it wore nothing blinding: brooches of undue length, swords, canes, mountain climbers' pickaxes, lighted lamps in hats, tame magpies . . . or nothing deafening: the din of a drum-and-bugle call, transistor radios, firecrackers, etc., but that each person deck himself out as he wished in order to be receptive to the maximum degree to the play being performed on stage: the audience has the right to be mad. The more serious the play, the greater may be the audience's need to affront it adorned, and even masked.

One ought to be able to enter and leave during the performance, without bothering anyone. And remain standing too, and even walk up to the stage if one feels like it, the way one approaches a painting, or steps back away from it. Thus if *The Screens* were being performed at this period, a certain space would have to be reserved directly on-stage for a certain number of walk-ons – silent and motionless – who would be part of the audience, having donned costumes designed by the costume designer – the notables on one side of the stage, and the common-law convicts on the other, masked and in chains, guarded by armed gendarmes.

☐ While I was writing this play, I pictured it as being performed in an open-air theatre in which the tiers of seats, carved out of the side of a hill, would be mere earthen benches. The stage at the bottom of the hill, and the sets (the screens) standing out against the trees of a full-grown forest.

☐ There should be added to the text of *The Screens* something approximating a score. This is within the realm of possibility. The director, taking into account the various tonal qualities of the different actors' voices, will have to invent a manner of speaking which ranges from murmurs to shouts. Sentences, a tempest of sentences, must be delivered like so many howls, others will be warbles, still others will be delivered in a normal conversational tone.

☐ The director will decide what the Mother's barking noises should be – which will be very different from what Leila's should be. The same will hold true for Scene Fourteen. It will be the job of the actors on-stage to convey the thunder and the sound of the rain.

☐ How will the drawings be done? The actors will have to be taught. Using coloured chalk, they ought to achieve some really festive effects on the screens. Even the drawings of the mountains of Giant Cedars, or of the Big Dipper: everything ought to be painted with care, the aim being to move the audience. Even if the drawings are unskilful, awkward, naïve, the actors ought to put as much effort and concentration into doing them as they put into their acting.

The clock drawn by Leila will be a very handsome model of a Louis XV or Louis XIV clock, or even rococo, full of scrolls, flowers, etc.

☐ A good deal of black material will have to be used for the costumes, to set off the other colours. The 'background' of this play is black. I wonder why?

☐ The props: the wheelbarrow, cheese grater, bicycle, gloves, etc., will also be interpreted. Larger than life, made of stronger material (the cheese grater out of cast iron), heavier, in order to command attention successfully in a space as big as this stage. In certain places they may be encircled with a black line, or their shadow traced on the ground, or on one of the screens by an actor, etc. The reason for this being to lend the moment a certain density. In short, treat everything as a joke.

☐ Each scene, and each section within a scene, must be perfected and played as rigorously and with as much discipline as if it were a short play, complete in itself. Without any smudges. And without there being the slightest suggestion that another scene, or section within a scene, is to follow those that have gone before.

□ In the twelfth scene, the Arabs ought to make their drawings very quickly; but some of them must dally, and even a chosen few come back – even twice or three times in succession – to the screen with their chalk and their charcoal to put a final touch, to emphasise a shadow, etc.

Another Letter to Roger Blin

This is how I see certain costumes and make-up.

☐ *The Mother* – Her hair of tow. A white face, made up with ceruse, and very elaborate wrinkles – blue, mauve, purple – from the eyes to the temples, from the wings of the nose to the mouth and down around the chin; finally, the tendons of the neck made very prominent. Her hands as white as her head, and the wrinkles, or rather the veins, extremely visible. The same for her legs, up to her knees. As for her eyes, not too large and not too oriental.

The dress, which is very heavy, comes down to just below her feet, so that the Mother has to lift it slightly in order to walk. The dress is made of rags from various cloths, of a variety of forms and materials, in different shades of purple and mauve. The seams will be visible, the rags having been pieced together with a coarse white thread.

☐ *Kadidja* – Her face purple, almost black. The colour of Negroes' lips, more or less. Her wrinkles, which are numerous, will be white. I think they ought to start at the wings of the nose and move towards the hair, the ears, and the chin. Her hands, her lower arms, and her legs, made-up the same way.

She will use her black umbrella, sometimes closed, sometimes open, but patched together.

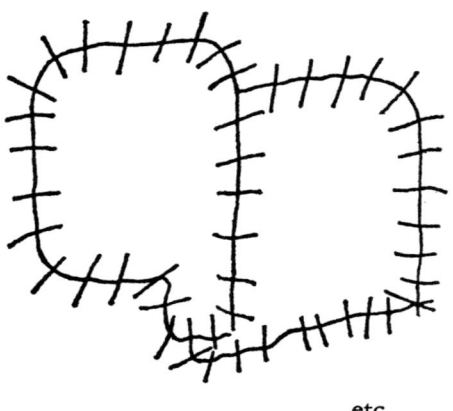

Of course, the drawings on the backs of the pages must be interpreted by you. You may well have different ideas about the dresses and make-up.

etc.

Her dress will be yellow. Every possible yellow, a patchwork of saffron, ochre, etc. Yellow even when she goes to mourn the dead. But it's a dress that can be raised belt high, over a long petticoat, dragging on the ground, perhaps of dark blue material. (Talk this over with Madame Acquart.)

White hair, but stiff, drawn back.

☐ All the other women will have umbrellas and will be dressed in the same way, with skirts made out of yellow or greenish rags.

☐ *Ommu* – White hair that falls down over her shoulders. She's the crazy one of the three. White hair, very white.

A dress made out of sacking; if you like, a kind of very rough gunny sack. Cut into an assemblage of pieces, like the others' dresses. But this time with a very full skirt and a sort of train that she will hold up with the hand she is not using to hold her cane. She is wearing shoes with very high heels. She has to be taller than Saïd.

Her face will be yellow, beset by an infinite number of small wrinkles in among the very large and very dark (brown) circular wrinkles which will make her face look like a full moon, if possible covered with craters and lunar seas like the Sea of Serenity. Get a photograph, very much enlarged, of the surface of the moon. Ask for one from the National Aeronautics and Space Administration. The same holds true for her legs and arms: holes and monticules.

☐ *Warda* – Her face completely white. She is painted in the presence of the audience. I see her green. In a big white petticoat, not patched together from many different pieces but cut out of some good material, perhaps pink. A gilded greatcoat will be draped over her. Like a cope of the Blessed Sacrament. Heavy, gilded ankle-boots. If possible made out of cast iron. Her hair sky-blue. A chignon set very high on her head. Like the chignon Marie Antoinette wore before she went to prison. Very high. Full of hat pins. Gilded make-up, or something akin. Golden hands. Don't bother your head too much about Algeria.

Warda's teeth: false. Buck teeth with plenty of gold, like Saïd's. And like those that Leila will have.

☐ I've forgotten the names of the other women, except that of the widow Germain. Her, you should sweeten up. She has two teeth left: one in the upper left part of the mouth, one in the lower right part. Her lips sunken. Work on her face, with diagonal wrinkles, in such a way as to form diamond shapes. Turn-of-the-century dress. Blonde hair, with ringlets: as cute as can be.

☐ *Saïd* – I'm tired. In any case, make his ears stick out even more, and his mouth more flabbergasted.

☐ Make all the actors work. I have the impression that they think they can do anything. It's imperative that they be taken completely aback, in accordance with the meaning of the term as you see it.
  All best,

Jean Genet

☐ Actually, I think that we should look for make-up, and for gestures and movements to go with it, of a much more evil sort. I've really been far too timid.

Genet

Another Letter

This is the way, my dear Roger, I have seen the first part of the play.

The following I have found admirable:
What you have done
Maria Casarès
Paulette Annen
Amidou
Madeleine Renaud (very young, perfect)
Jean-Louis Barrault
Cattand
Kerjean
Weber
Granval (he's made enormous strides)
The couple who pins
Alric
Rousselet shows great promise.

There is very little one can tell them by way of direction. I think that they will find within themselves, as they rehearse, the means to perfect their roles.

This still leaves the others: let's not talk about them for the moment.

For the notable, find a kid eighteen years old, with a squarely clipped white beard and artificially white hair. The young actor made up as an old man will have to fabricate attitudes of old age. Otherwise, it's hopeless.

A rule which in any event must not be broken:

The Man, the Woman, the attitude and the word which in real life seem abject, in the theatre must fill the audience with wonder, without exception, must always astonish by their elegance and their obviousness.

Nothing on-stage, nothing that ought to be ugly or ridiculous, of course.

Perhaps you ought to take aside those whose names I have mentioned to you and make full use of them to enhance the play – and therefore themselves.

Try, in spite of everything, to lead them toward a more hieratical theatre. Otherwise, ARSENIC.

Or hit them. I can't send you a team of wrestlers to wipe them out. But *they already are!*

Two pages of notes follow.

Notes

Saïd's first shout ends, or is uttered, as a statement. *It shouldn't be*. He ought to raise his voice and leave it suspended: Not Ro*se*! but R*o*se!

☐ He makes two or three gestures that are not voluntary, but submitted to. Gestures which sustain *quite naturally* the spoken word. These gestures lessen his verbal and gesticulatory impact.

☐ When he lets his hands fall back onto his thighs we can hear it in the audience. This is disturbing. We should hear nothing at all when he claps his hands and strikes his thighs.

We should not hear anything, even when the crowd runs across the stage, especially not the sound of the floorboards.

Nor should we hear anything when the Mouth strikes the floor to call the dead – or else we should hear something else, an atomic explosion if you can manage it, I'd much prefer that.

☐ When the Mouth answers the Mother, who asks him if it's time, Jean-Louis Barrault ought to fish out his wristwatch and dangle it in her direction, but without looking at it himself.

□ Sir Harold's son ought not to lower his head when he tells his father 'yes' (in response to his father's question about whether he is armed), but raise it.

□ In the scene of the dead, when the Mother upbraids the women, I wonder whether she ought not to clench her fists as she stretches them out, rather than hold them open.
Open hands are more the symbol of entreaty. In any case, since she does it twice, I think she ought to have her hands open at first, then clenched the second time.

□ In prison:
Remove the Voice once and for all. The text is too flat.

□ My purpose in writing this passage was to recreate the prison. I haven't succeeded in finding the proper tone.

□ Leila should greet the Gendarme before her line: 'I'm Saïd's wife.' First the curtsy.

□ The yapping of the two women, mother and daughter, very pretty, but when she comes, before barking in support of her mother, Leila must smell her out: then yap with her. Then against her, etc.

□ Maria Casarès hasn't learned how to rest in the paroxysm: she's going to be exhausted. But she is so beautiful in her exhaustion!

LETTERS TO ROGER BLIN

☐ Very good, the Mouth's differences of tone. His voice suddenly fresh and young when he answers as Slimane. But be careful about his age; sometimes, before his fatigue, or feigned fatigue, the deep voice returns. If Jean-Louis Barrault can rid himself entirely of his Parisian tone of voice, in the role of Slimane, he would be magnificent.

☐ The Mother does not hunt for the gravestone with a sufficient display of myopia. She ought to make a greater show of making out the names on the graves.

☐ You've cut the story about the cork oak trees and the sawdust corks. Why? I was rather fond of it.

☐ The two colonists, seated, ought to be back to back, not side by side.

The two preceding pages are some suggestions offered with a view towards rectifying, but the play taken as a whole is astonishing. That you have understood the play as I desired is not surprising, for you are quick to understand and discriminating, but you have had the talent and tenacity to apply your understanding. I would have liked to dissociate myself from this performance: I no longer have the strength to do so. Your spiderlike patience and the degree to which you have succeeded have ensnared me in your web. The job done by the actors and actresses whose names I have mentioned, under your direction, I consider as a personal tribute. I am quite happy, and a trifle ashamed at being so.

In *The Blacks*, the text of which was more carefully prepared as to its effect, your work amazed me less. In any case, it seems to me that I was as much responsible for its success as were you. In *The Screens*, the full credit goes to you. If I had thought that the play could be performed, I would have made it more beautiful – or a complete failure. Without touching it, you have taken it and made it light. It's very beautiful. You have my friendship, and my admiration.

Jean

There are still many things that need to be said, but they slip my mind.

You and Barrault must have cut a great deal. It seemed to

me a trifle skimpy. You mustn't be afraid to breathe, and to know that we have a whole life ahead of us in which to put on this play. The audience will follow what you have done quite naturally. If it is well done, you won't bore anyone.

Another Letter with Notes

Dear Roger,
   Another couple of notes.

☐ The Gendarme's explosion is not violent enough. After the exchange of the '*tu*'s' and '*vous*'s' there ought to be a slight calm, and a silence, then, without any warning, the mad explosion of the Gendarme, frothing at the mouth, drivelling, etc. But in general he is perfect.

☐ For each Arab soldier who is going to draw, you should invent a manner of walking which is constantly new: one walks forward with his hands in his pockets, lightly brushing the screens as he sways back and forth; another is full of determination; still another dragging one foot behind him; another dancing the java and having a good time, etc., and always Kadidja, motionless, never looking at the soldiers when she summons them, since she is dead.

☐ Give Sir Harold some directions: he is caught red-handed. It is possible that he gets out of the difficulty.

☐ Too frequently the actors look out at the audience. I think they ought to look at it without seeing it. In any case, when they do look out at the audience, they are wrong to look constantly at the orchestra seats. If, God forbid, they really feel compelled to look at it, then let them take the meaningful step of casting their eyes all the way up to the top galleries.

☐ When Saïd alludes to the purchase of Leila from her father, he can chant his lines a little more than he does. A pretence of foolishness can help him to appear meaner.

☐ Try to shift, to unbalance to some degree, the voice and acting of the woman mourner who talks for such a long time with the Mother (I don't know her name). Make her stutter, and see how that works. Have her bring her voice down two or three tones. She is too sober, too composed. Too good.

☐ Work on the *Theft* (the scene preceding Saïd's release from prison). Too distinguished a theft. I would like it to be a little Neapolitan.

☐ That seems to be all I have to suggest. What you have done is magnificent.

All best,

Jean

When the actors walk, run, jump through the doors or windows, they – or most of them – sound like a herd of elephants. Without creating the perceptible silence of nocturnal burglars or of ladies who stoop down to peek through keyholes at their maids, I should like the actors to make no sound with their feet in order to replace it, if I may suggest, by a ringing sound similar to that made by my cane one day in Maria Casarès' living room when it struck the slender leg of a metal table. Therefore, silence to start with, in order to enable me to invent unexpected noises.

In the same way, don't let the Arab worker light a cigarette: the match flame not being able to be *imitated* on stage; a lighted match, in the audience or elsewhere, is the same as on-stage. To be avoided.

☐ There are times when certain actors remain on-stage too long. One of the few expressions of theatrical jargon that I've remembered – but remembered clearly – is this: they are hamming it up.

The actor must act quickly, even in his slowness, but his speed, lightninglike, will amaze. That and his acting will make him so beautiful that, when he is snatched up by the emptiness of the wings, the audience will experience a feeling of sadness, a kind of regret: they will have seen a meteor loom into view and pass by. This kind of acting will give life to the actor and to the play.

Therefore: appear, shine, and, as it were, die.

☐ At first no one knows anything. The actors have little knowledge, but the man who is teaching them must know nothing and learn everything, about himself and his art, as he teaches them. It will be a discovery for them but also for him.

☐ It seems to me that the public does not know how to listen. It tends to confuse two words: one hears with both one's ears, but one listens – or strains one's ears – with one's toes.

☐ If I wanted the stage bathed in bright light, it was to keep each actor from covering up his errors, his fleeting mistakes, his fatigue, or his indifference, in a redeeming darkness. Of course, this much light will hurt him, but to be so brightly lighted will perhaps compel him.

☐ While on the subject of lighting: it will be a good idea if each actor, by his performance, casts light on the other or others who, in turn, will cast their light on him. The stage will therefore be a site not where reflections spend themselves but where bursts of light meet and collide. It would by the same token be a site where Christian charity amused itself.

Notes Sent to Roger Blin on April 14

Don't forget! All the make-up extremely violent, but all *asymmetrical*.

☐ For the young man who draws the revolvers on the screen: he must roll his sleeve up to his elbow, step back from the screen, so that only his hand and arm that are drawing are visible against the screen. The hand very heavily made up, so as to be visible.

☐ The second young man: he will draw with short, angry strokes, doing an equally angry dance directly in front of the screen. – The heart to be drawn: it is the Sacred Heart of Jesus, with flames in place of the aorta. – Use surgeon's gloves, made-up: a make-up of black gloves and red blood.

☐ Do the entrance of the Paratroopers over again: the first time, with the Lieutenant:
  The Eucharistic Host and Latin, etc.
at one point the Lieutenant must turn around with a worried air, and the other Paratroopers must follow suit; they are walking backwards, stooped over, afraid of the night.

☐ The Arabs who draw:
  the first one stands behind Kadidja and holds out his open hands in front of himself and in front of her (he says he is holding revolvers);
  after he has raised his right sleeve, he begins to draw with rapid strokes.
  He steps back from his drawing the way a real painter would.

☐ The Arab who draws the horns dances with a swaying motion over next to Kadidja, his hands behind his back.
  They must all be happy.

☐ Ommu's performance:
  She overpoeticises. You know what I mean.
  She ought to be less declamatory when she delivers the line where I say something to the effect: 'It's the useless ideas that have to be protected and provoke song.' This should be said very softly. While she runs.
  When she wants her aspirin:
    'My as——pirin!'
  the way an addict calls for his heroin.

Notes Sent to Roger Blin on April 15

Immediately replace the screen depicting the orange trees by a bare screen of one colour, the dark blue of night, on which the Arabs will draw very vivid flames.

☐ Think about suggesting to the Arab soldiers, at the very end, that before they fire at Saïd they ought to stoop down and look for him beneath the stage doors and windows as though they were looking in a thicket.

☐ If Ommu uses crutches, it would be a good idea to cover them with bright red velvet, in tatters, and for Ommu to use them like knitting needles, as though she were knitting on the ground.

☐ For Ommu: have her deliver her line at the end with impatience: 'It's the unimportant things that have to live.' The quote is approximate, since I don't have the text. She must say the line with impatience, anger, clarity, irritation. Not the pompous way Merleau-Ponty would have said it.

☐ A slightly faster pace for Sir Harold and Blankensee.

Another Letter

My dear Roger,

Since we are in agreement on this point – that the twenty performances which have already taken place* constitute only an approach of the play, or, if you like, a series of rehearsals – it is imperative that we review what works and what does not.

About the actors' performances: do I have to repeat myself? Saturday night, Maria [Casarès] was dazzling. I'm fully aware that it isn't, and will not be, Saturday every day, but she should be encouraged to maintain that brilliance. That evening she was a great tragic actress. Paulette is still working on her part, and will continue to do so; leave her alone. Barrault projected a tone that was moving, and gave a performance he ought to repeat in September. Even if in the beginning he was groping, the four or five last evenings he played Madani and Si Slimane superbly. Above all, let him maintain this attitude which is not absolutely safe.

That's it: it is imperative that no one have an attitude, or a series of gestures, which are perfectly safe. Barrault is constantly unstable, fragile, and unbreakable. I should like him too, like

---

* The first twenty performances of *The Screens* were given at the Théâtre de France in the spring of 1966. After the customary summer break, further performances were given during the autumn. The present undated letter was obviously written immediately after the last performance given in the spring.—*Tr.*

Casarès, Madeleine Renaud, and Kerjean, to be an example of strength and delicacy. An example, too, of theatrical meticulosity: he knows how to make-up his fingers and toes, and he takes the time to do it. Some evening take Amidou into Barrault's dressing room without any advance warning when he's making up his hands. For Madeleine – Barrault is right – we need a wig in disarray for the gunfire in the whorehouse. And let her play the perspiring baker's wife who's selling her bread like hot cakes.

But! What does not work? I can't say I'm pleased with the screens. If Acquart doesn't get bloody mad, we're done for. For the first screen: it's a tall palm tree, on a white or blue background, that has to be made to move. And all the others will be redone. Make it very clear to Acquart that the first problem is to understand what a screen is, and only then to decorate it.

Madame Acquart has made superb costumes, but for Christ's sake why is Alric dressed in hand-me-downs? And what about the soldiers? Michel Creton was right when he said to me: 'We ought to be sexy too.' The soldiers ought to have costumes cut and decorated like the Sergeant's, if you agree with the basic premise of wanting an already handsome Sergeant to be even more impressive. As for his acting (the Sergeant's), I was wrong to tell him to smile as soon as he made his first appearance on-stage. In the first part, before he breaks the screen of the dead, he ought to be a mean son of a bitch.

Each soldier will have, in addition to his accoutrements and make-up, an attitude which is his alone, a made-up attitude, which will not be the same for everyone. You have to show it to them. No pockets on the knees. The Lieutenant will be far more dazzling if he is in charge of dazzling troops. Therefore, sexy soldiers, not rank rookies in fatigues.

Weber has succeeded in finding a very pretty make-up.

So has Creton. But what about the others? You ought to draw it for them.

That's not all. Madame Acquart must remake Djemila's costume. (You can see that I'm making notes as the random thoughts occur to me.)

When the General rolls down the depths of time, have him pivot slowly, then faster and faster, the way a stone falls faster and faster, until the final impact, attaining, if he can, the speed of light.

The little drawing boxes – or pistols, as the utensils into which the weak and infirm piss are called – are very ugly. And what is worse, these pistols restrict the actors from making the gestures we would like: ample. Can't Acquart find another technique? The actors looked as though they were pissing off the stump of their forearm.

The idea of silken flames that rise and descend is very nice, but not out of orange trees that look like strawberry bushes. Against a background of night. Strawberry bushes!

Yes indeed, even if I'm satisfied. Rousselet has some more work cut out for him: more nervy, more of a bastard, and when he breaks through the screen he will have at last, on his coolly trained eye, his crown of periwinkles on his crossed eye. When he gives his account of his death, let him take his time. The public will listen.

And the farts? I refuse to give them up. Have you given up farting?

An important point: when Alric, well-dressed this time, does his belly dance, he ought to back off the stage, with his face to the audience, into the wing opposite from that into which Leila escaped flat on her belly. The public will not be fazed, even if it misunderstands; and, to take an example, let the Gendarme get lost on a false lead.

Cattand tends to look out at the audience too much. He

also ought to address his soldiers, or stare into space, or do anything that crosses his mind. But nothing else in the way he acts should be changed, for it is all perfect. And I might add: perfect at the right time.

I'm getting to the point: you must make Marcelle Ranson work. She's ready and willing. She must have crutches with narrow strips of purple velvet wrapped around them. I really insist on this. Have her modulate the text more than she does. She'll know how to do it, but damn it, have someone work with her!

There are too many laughs in this play. Many ought to be silent, simply the soldiers' grinning faces. Or whistles. I leave it up to you to find the appropriate moments. You can very easily have the men and women whistle rather than laugh wholeheartedly. And what about the orchestration of laughter which I spoke to you about?

The Mother's farmyard is not varied enough: let the others help Maria and Paulette. The young actors could crow like roosters in the wings.

Another detail: when Saïd reappears on-stage, he will be wearing a new costume, made of purple rags.

☐ Madeleine Renaud will come on-stage in the second scene from the wings, borne on the first step of a stepladder, and when Saïd – who will be invisible to the audience – arrives, she, clothed in the bishop's mantel, will ascend to the fourth or fifth step, and then finally to the top of the stepladder and, perched in this manner, she will leave the stage at the same time as the screen depicting the whorehouse from which the Arabs, who have just come and are fully satisfied, will emerge.

The dressmaker's dummy on which Warda's coat is draped

is extremely ugly, to my mind. Acquart ought to make a new one.

☐ The Arabs' quaking in the presence of Sir Harold's son: you need to work on this some more. Every actor must practice making all his limbs tremble in such a way that they all provide a painful vision of fear. They will tremble from head to toe, from their shoulders to their hands, and the trembling should be carried to trancelike lengths but should, in passing, evoke the image of a field of rye swayed by a strong wind, or the flight of a flock of partridges. Does that mean anything to you?

☐ The actors playing the roles of Arabs could, if they are not too lazy, do something clever with their hair, either curl it, or put some kind of oily hair tonic on it, or some sticky substance, etc. There are many ways to make adolescent hairdos expressive, but, damn it, are these kids going to agree to work in front of a mirror not as gigolos but as actors?

☐ The few demonstrators of the Occident group* – 'In the deserted Occident what became of my boredom . . .' – give in to the lazy side of their nature when they see on-stage a dead

---

* Performances were interrupted on two occasions. The incidents were caused by a group of some fifteen or so first-year cadets from the French Military Academy of St.-Cyr. The first evening degenerated into a general riot, and on the second, sixteen members of the audience were arrested, but the play finally continued. Later, the Public Relations Committee of the Indochinese and Algerian Ex-Servicemen's League issued a proclamation calling on the people of Paris to stage a demonstration and to demand that *The Screens* be banned.—*Tr.*

French officer sniffing the meticulous farts of his soldiers, whereas they ought to be seeing actors playing at being or at seeming. . . . Actors' acting is to military reality what smoke bombs are to the reality of napalm.

☐ They're the ones who are the real corrupters of the army, for if they read the word 'chancre' in the dictionary they cannot help seeing chancres sprouting on all the military pricks transmitting chancres to all the tricolour asses. Now, they have read only seven letters, and because of them off they go to war. What a worrisome West!

☐ This may not be an original thought with me, but let me restate it anyway, that the patron saint of actors is Tiresias, because of his dual nature. Legend has it that he retained the male sex for seven years, and for seven more the other. For seven years a man's clothing, for seven a woman's. In a certain way, at certain moments – or perhaps always – his femininity followed in close pursuit of his virility, the one or the other being constantly asserted, with the result that he never had any rest, I mean any specific place where he could rest. Like him, the actors are neither this nor that, and they must be aware that they are a presence constantly beset by femininity or its opposite, but ready to play to the point of abasement that which, be it virility or its opposite, is in any case predetermined.

Saint Tiresias, the patron saint of actors.

As for the divinatory powers of the saint, let every actor make an effort to see clearly within himself.

Of course I am completely ignorant when it comes to the theatre in general, but I do know enough about my own.

Whenever a judge passes a sentence, let us demand that he be prepared other than by knowledge of the criminal code. Vigils, fasting, prayer, an attempted suicide or murder, could all contribute to making the sentence he is going to pass an event so momentous – I mean a poetic event – that he, the judge, having rendered it, will be completely exhausted, on the verge of rendering his soul either unto death or madness. Bloodless, voiceless, he would take two or three years to recover. This is a great deal to ask of a judge. But what about us? We are still a long way from the poetic act. All of us – you, me, the actors – must steep ourselves for a long time in the shadows, we must work until we are utterly worn out, so that one evening we come to the brink of the final act. And we must make many mistakes, and profit from them. The fact is that we still have a long way to go, and for this play neither madness nor death seems to me to be the fairest sanction. And yet it is these twin goddesses that we must move in order that they may turn their attention to us. No, we are in no danger of death, nor has poetry come the way it should.

If I wanted what you had promised me, bright lights, it was so that each actor would *finish* his gestures or lines brilliantly and would rival the brightest of lights. I also wanted the house lights to be on: with the collective ass of the audience scrunched down in its seats, its immobility imposed by the acting – that was enough to make a distinction between the stage and that house, but the lights are necessary for complicity to be established. A poetic act, not a spectacle, even were it beautiful in the normal sense of the term, would have taken place. Only Maria Casarès, because of her own innate ability, performed brilliantly the last evening.

In another letter, which you have probably lost, I told you that my books, like my plays, were written against myself. You know what I mean. Among other things, this: the soldier scenes are meant to exalt – and I mean *exalt* – the Army's prime, its chief, virtue: stupidity. Real paratroopers have given me a hard-on; I've never had an erection over stage paratroopers. And if I do not succeed through the text itself to expose myself, then you have to help me. Against myself, against ourselves, whenever these performances put us on God knows what decent side into which poetry fails to penetrate.

We have to consider that we have failed. Our fault lies in having lost our nerve, collapsing like a bagpipe which deflates as it emits a few sounds that we would like to think are attractive, and in our yielding to the illusion that the finished melody was well worth the loss of precious air. By small, successive stages we have slowly but surely turned the play into something insipid. Successive stages in order to make certain we would have a success which, to my mind, is in the final analysis a failure.

Jacques Maglia said to me: 'Everything takes place as though the two of you, Blin and yourself, were proud as peacocks. Instead of a play which should stagger you when it is over, its seeming success reassures you.'

I surrendered on several occasions to Barrault's objections, and to your own. Your knowledge of the theatre threatens to make you avoid any errors of taste; my ignorance of this same profession should have led me towards them.

I am not maintaining that the *written* text of the play is of any great value, but I can assure you that I did not, for example, look down on any of my characters – be it Sir Harold, the Gendarme, or the Paratroopers. You can be sure that I have never tried to 'understand' them, but, having created them, on paper and for the stage, I do not want to deny them. What binds me to them is something other than irony or contempt. They also help to shape me. I have never copied life – an event or a man, the Algerian War or colonialists – but life has, quite naturally, caused various images to come to life within me, or has illuminated them if they were already there – images which I have translated either by a character or an act. Pascal Monod, one of the students of the military, said to me after the last performance that the Army is not as much of a caricature as I have made it out. I did not have time then to answer him that what we are dealing with here is a dream army, a dream roughly sketched out on paper and, poorly or well, brought to fruition on a stage, which might be wooden and whose flooring creaks beneath one's footsteps.

Let us come back to the lighting. I'm sure you clearly understand that this way of playing with darkness, semi-darkness, and light is a recourse, delightful and chilly, which gives the spectator the time to go into raptures or to regain his composure. I wanted the ice floe, the promised land which blinds and is unremitting. What ever happened to that white, metallic material that Acquart once talked to us about and which, according to my instructions, should have constituted the very material wherein the actors moved and had their being? Will it be possible for you to use this mysterious, Mallarméan, and allegorical material, even if only a for a single evening's performance?

People don't go off to wage war if they don't love it, if they don't feel themselves made for – or, if you wish, destined for – combat. The same holds true for the theatre. The actors, too much at ease on-stage, relax between their brief appearances, or, rather, crowd against one another around the blaring television in the actors' dressing room. Certain canons read their breviaries at vespers while their minds are a thousand miles away preoccupied with God knows what, but twenty-year-old actors should not be canons. Even when she is off-stage, Maria Casarès remains in the wings, attentive or exhausted, but present: the others get the hell away as fast as they can. They could at least have the courtesy to listen to what their fellow actors are saying on-stage. By dialing some buttons they tune out the voices coming from the stage, bearing with them bravura or weariness, failure or cleverness, and they are watching television. They are listening to it. Instead of leaving the world, they bring it back, as though the stage were a place of perdition. Young actors are remarkable in that they are no sooner on-stage than they do all in their power to conceal themselves, to dissolve into a grisaille of words and movements. Can't you tell them that to glitter too brightly in their daily lives off-stage prevents a long contained brilliance from exploding and illuminating the stage? Even if they have only one line to deliver, one gesture to make, that line and gesture ought to contain whatever luminous quality each actor bears within himself which has been waiting for a long time for this magic moment: to be on-stage. Surely every actor must be encouraged to be – were it only for the duration of a single appearance, lightning-like and true – of such beauty that his disappearance into the wings will literally break the audience's heart. And that the public, though it remains under the spell of what succeeds his exit, will still miss him after he is gone.

Finally, if I am so insistent about the bright lights, both the stage and house lights, it is because I should in some way like both actors and audience to be caught up in the same illumination, and for there to be no place for them to hide, or even half-hide.

These are the few notes, my dear Roger, that the production of *The Screens* and my friendship for you compelled me to make.

J. G.

Final Letter

I wrote to Maria Casarès to tell her more or less the following: 'When you are explaining the situation to Saïd: "You take the least expensive . . . you and she take each other, etc.," I think that you should try these gestures: with each of your hands raised on either side of your face, and not supported by your knees, form a circle with your thumb and forefinger, more or less the way a lecturer does.

'And then, at the line: "You take each other . . ." make both your hands point in one direction, away from Saïd.'

☐ If I am recalling this direction, it is so that you will better understand why, when we first started rehearsals, I forbade anyone to make the slightest gesture, however simple, with their body or their little finger. It seemed to me indispensable that the actors' voice expressed first, and by itself, as a notion of its body, the entire character. The fact is that actors are always prone to 'finding spontaneously' gestures which help the words to emerge from the mouth. This – gestures and voice used in a banal way (according to the basic meaning of 'banal') – results in a kind of useless redundancy. It is preferable, when the voice has found its true inflections, to discover the gestures which will then reinforce it, gestures which will no longer be familiarly granted the voice but will, perhaps, be in opposition to it – for example, to an inflection of deep regret a very light-hearted gesture of the hand and foot – in such a way that the whole forms a long succession of unstipulated agreements – broken but always harmonious, freeing the actor from the temptation of the commonplace.

This procedure, a refusal of a natural sham, must not be carried out haphazardly: its goal, among other things, is to reveal and make heard what *generally* passes unperceived. Its real goal, of course, is a new joy, a new festivity, and God knows what besides.

We were therefore lucky that a flamboyant temperament agreed to give this method a try. I was very much afraid of hurting Maria Casarès when I asked her, for example, to look at herself in a mirror, to make faces in it without indulgence, and to discover, in this new uglified face, a beauty that every spectator – not the public, but every spectator – could find within himself in some faltering way, buried but capable of rising to its own surface.

Perhaps by other means, without erasing the famous actress, and perhaps aided by you, but in any case with a great deal of courage, Maria has attained her and my own goal.

If this short book opens with your name, you will surely understand that I wanted to close it with the name of this admirable woman, who has constantly helped you with her Iberian fire and passion: Maria Casarès.

Jean Genet

The Screens was first performed at the Théâtre de France on April 21, 1966, by the Jean-Louis Barrault – Madeleine Renaud Company. The sets and costumes were by André Acquart.

THE CHARACTERS*
(*in order of appearance*)

SAÏD	Amidou
THE MOTHER	Maria Casarès
WARDA	Madeleine Renaud
MALIKA	Annie Bertin
THE MAID	Claudie Bourlon
MUSTAPHA	André Batisse
AHMED	Yan Davrey
BRAHIM	Victor Béniard
LEILA	Paule Annen
SIR HAROLD	Paul Descombes
HABIB	Jean-Pierre Granval
TALEB	François Hélie
CHIGHA	Christiane Carpentier
KADIDJA	Germaine Kerjean
NEDJMA	Sylvia Moreau

* This cast of 62 characters follows the Théâtre de France production. The play, as originally written and published, has a cast of 98 characters. —*Tr.*

HABIBA	Micheline Uzan
SI SLIMANE (Madani-The Mouth)	Jean-Louis Barrault
THE GENDARME	Jacques Alric
MR. BLANKENSEE	Régis Outin
MALIK	Georges Sellier
ABDIL	Michel Bringuier
THE GUARD	Robert Lombard
THE LIEUTENANT	Gabriel Cattand
THE SERGEANT	Bernard Rousselet
PIERRE	André Weber
ROGER	Dominique Santarelli
JOJO	Michel Creton
PRESTON	Éric Gérard
WALTER	Michel Lebret
HERNANDEZ	Jean-Jacques Domenc
MORALES	Michel Berger
FELTON	Christian Jaulin
BRANDINESCHI	Pierre Benedetti
MRS. BLANKENSEE	Marie-Hélène Dasté
THE CHIEF	Jean-Guy Henneveux
THE PHOTOGRAPHER	Xavier Bellanger
THE VAMP	Tania Torrens
THE ACADEMICIAN	Michel Bertay
THE GENERAL	Jean-Roger Tandou
THE BANKER	Jacques Alric
THE COMMUNICANT	Brigitte Carva
THE SOLDIER	Luis Masson
THE MAN	François Hélie
THE WOMAN	Jeanne Martel
SIR HAROLD'S SON	François Gabriel
SALEM	Paul Descombes
NACEUR	Pierre Gallon
M'BAREK	Michel Dariel

LETTERS TO ROGER BLIN

LAHUSSEIN	Louis Frémont
SRIRA	Jean-Claude Amyl
LARBI	Patrice Chapelain-Midy
FIRST COMBATANT	Christian Pailhé
SECOND COMBATANT	Christian Bujeau
AMER	Alain Hitier
ABDESSELEM	Guy Didier
THE GENDARME'S WIFE	Catherine Rethi
DJEMILA	Michèle Oppenot
OMMU	Marcelle Ranson
NESTOR	Luis Masson
LALLA	Jane Martel
AZIZA	Céline Salles
AICHA	Marie-Claude Fuzier

The strange word Urb...

Whether the strange word 'urbanism' comes from some Pope Urban or from the Latin root for the word 'city', it will probably no longer have anything to do with the dead. The living will dispose of their corpses, surreptitiously or otherwise, the same way one gets rid of some shameful thought. By dispatching them to the crematorium oven, the urbanised world will deprive itself of one important theatrical mainstay, and perhaps even of the theatre itself. In place of the cemetery, the perhaps eccentric centre of the city, you will have columbariums with chimneys, without chimneys, with or without smoke, and the dead, burnt to a crisp like little calcinated loaves of bread, will be used as fertilizer for the kolkhozes and kibbutzim located some distance from the city. Still, if cremation takes some dramatic turn – either that one man were to be solemnly burnt or roasted alive, or that the City or State should desire to rid itself as it were in one fell swoop of some other community – the crematorium, like that of Dachau, evoking some very possible future architecturally outside of time, of the past as well as the future, its smokestack constantly maintained by cleaning crews who, as they circle this oblique erect sex of pink brick, sing lieder or whistle Mozart melodies perfectly in tune, who tend the open maw of this oven on whose grates ten or twelve bodies can be handled at once, then it may be possible for the theatre to survive, but if in the cities the crematoria are done away with or reduced to the size of some family grocery store, then the theatre will die. We shall ask future city planners to provide for a cemetery within the confines of the city, where the dead will continue to be buried, or to plan for a disturbing columbarium, a structure whose style will be simple yet impressive, and close beside it, in its shadow so to speak, or among the very graves, the theatre will be built. Do you see what I am driving at? The theatre will be built as close as possible to, actually in the guardian shadow of, the place where the dead are buried, or the solitary monument which digests them.

I'm offering you this advice without ceremony or undue solemnity; I'm dreaming rather, with the active nonchalance of a child who knows how important the theatre is.

☐ Among other things, the goal of the theatre is to take us outside the limits of what is generally referred to as 'historical' time but which is really theological. The moment the theatrical event begins, the time which will elapse no longer belongs to any calibrated calendar. It transcends the Christian era as it does the revolutionary era. Even if that time which is called 'historical' – I mean the time that flows from some mythical and controversial event, also known as Advent – does not disappear completely from the spectators' consciousness, another time, which each spectator lives to the full, then unfolds, and as it has neither beginning nor end, it destroys the historical conventions necessitated by social life, and at the same time destroys social conventions as well, not for the sake of just any disorder but neither for the sake of a liberation – the theatrical event being suspended, outside of historical time, on its own dramatic time – it is for the sake of a vertiginous liberation.

THE STRANGE WORD 'URB...'

By dint of duplicity, Western Christianity has done its best to ensnare all the peoples of the world in an era whose origin is purported to be some hypothetical Incarnation. What the West is trying to impose on the rest of the world, therefore, is quite simply what we might fairly refer to as the 'calendar coup'.

Trapped in a time named for, calculated from, an event that is of interest only to the West, the world is in serious danger, if it accepts this time, of emphasising it according to celebrations in which the whole world will be trapped.

It would therefore seem to be a matter of great urgency to multiply the number of 'Advents' from which calendars quite unrelated to those which are imposed imperialistically, can be established. I would even go so far as to say that any event, public or private, ought to give rise to a whole host of calendars, and in this way scuttle the Christian era and everything connected with this time reckoned from the Very Questionable Nativity.

The theatre . . .
THE THEATRE
THE THEATRE

☐ Where shall we go from here? Towards what form? The theatrical site, containing the stage and the auditorium?

The site. I told an Italian who wanted to build a theatre whose elements would be movable and whose architecture flexible, depending on what play was being performed – even before he had finished his sentence I said that the architecture of the theatre still remains to be discovered but that it must be stationary, immobilised, so that it can be held responsible: it shall be judged by its shape. It's too easy to put one's trust in the movable. Let anyone who wants to work towards the

THE STRANGE WORD 'URB...'

perishable, but only after the irreversible act by which we shall be judged or, if you prefer, the fixed act which judges itself has been accomplished.

☐ Because I am not blessed with spiritual powers – assuming they exist – I do not require that the theatrical site be chosen, after an attempt at meditation, by a man or a community capable of such an effort; and yet the fact remains that the architect must indeed discover the sense of the theatre in the world and, once having understood it, go about his work with an almost priestly and smiling solemnity. If necessary, let him be supported and protected during his undertaking by a group of men who know nothing about architecture but who are capable of real daring in the effort of meditation, that is of laughing inwardly.

☐ If we accept – for the time being – the commonly held notions of time and history, and if we also admit that the act of painting is no longer the same as it was before the invention of photography, then it would seem that the theatre will not remain the same as it was before the advent of the cinema and television. Going back as far as we can to the very origins of the theatre, it would seem that, in addition to its essential function, each play was crammed with concerns deriving from politics, religion, morality, or what have you, transforming the dramatic action into a didactic means of expression.

Perhaps – I shall always say perhaps because I am but a man and all alone – perhaps television and movies will better the role of education: then the theatre will find itself emptied, perhaps cleansed, of whatever encumbered it; perhaps it may shine brightly with its own inherent quality, or qualities – which perhaps remains, or remain, to be discovered.

THE STRANGE WORD 'URB...'

☐ With the exception of a handful of paintings – or fragments of paintings – few artists who painted before the discovery of photography have left us any tangible evidence of a vision and a kind of painting freed from the slavish concern of copying natural likenesses. Not daring to tamper to any great extent with the face – with the exception of Franz Hals (*The Regents*) – the painters daring enough to serve both the object painted and the painting (Velasquez, Rembrandt, Goya) used as a pretext a flower or a dress. It is possible that painters looked foolish when confronted with the results of photography. Afterwards they pulled themselves together and discovered what painting was all about.

In the same way, or in some similar fashion, playwrights have been taken aback and felt foolish in the light of the potentials of television and cinema. If they are able to accept the idea – assuming the idea is meaningful – that the theatre cannot compete with the extraordinary means which television and cinema have at their disposal, then those who write for the theatre will discover the virtues inherent in the theatre, virtues which, perhaps, derive only from myth.

☐ Politics, history, classical physiological demonstrations, an evening's light entertainment ought to give way to something else which I don't know quite how to describe but which I suspect will be more dazzling. All this dung, all this liquid manure will be eliminated. People will come to understand that slightly heated words are neither dung or liquid manure. I might point out, in passing, that these words and the situations they evoke occur so frequently in my plays primarily because they have been 'forgotten' in most other plays: words and situations that are termed vulgar or uncouth hurried to my plays, sought refuge in them where they were granted the right

THE STRANGE WORD 'URB...'

of sanctuary. If my theatre stinks, it is because the other smells so sweet.

☐ Drama, that is the theatrical act at the time of its performance, cannot be just anything, but it can take as its pretext anything it may choose. In fact, it seems to me that any event whatsoever, be it visible or invisible, can, if it is isolated, that is fragmented in the continuum, if it is well handled, serve as the pretext or even as the point of departure and arrival for the theatrical act. Any event we have experienced, in one way or another, whose burning we have felt, a burning caused by a fire which cannot only be extinguished if it is stirred up.

We will have nothing to do with politics, entertainment, morality, etc. If, in spite of ourselves, they slip into the theatrical act, let them be driven out until all trace of them is gone: they are the dross with which one can make a film, something for television, the comic strips, photo-novels – ah, there is a graveyard full of those old car bodies.

☐ But what about the drama? If its origin is some dazzling moment in the author's experience, it is up to him to seize this lightning and, beginning with the moment of illumination which reveals the void, to arrange a verbal architecture – that is, grammatical and ceremonial – slyly suggesting that from this void some semblance is snatched which reveals the void.

☐ Let us remark in passing that the posture of Christian prayer, with both eyes and head bowed, does not encourage meditation. It is a physical position which invokes an irresponsive and submissive intellectual attitude; it discourages any spiritual effort. If you choose this position, God can happen by, smite you on the nape of your neck, leave His mark which you have to live with for a long time to come. To meditate, you have to find an open attitude – not one of defiance – but not one of surrender to God. You have to be careful. Ever so slight a surrender, and God will bestow his Grace upon you: you're screwed.

☐ In today's cities, the only place – unfortunately still on the outskirts – where a theatre could be built is in the cemetery. The choice will be useful for both cemetery and theatre alike. The architect of the theatre will be unable to bear the inane constructions wherein families bury their dead.

Raze the chapels. Perhaps keep a few ruins: a piece of a column, a pediment, the wing of an angel, a broken urn, to suggest that a vengeful indignation has wrought this initial drama so that the vegetation, perhaps some handy grass as well, born from all of the rotting bodies, can level the field of the dead. If a site is reserved for the theatre, the public, when it arrives and leaves, ought to take paths which skirt the graves. Imagine for a moment what it would be like for the audience to leave after a performance of Mozart's *Don Giovanni*, making its way amongst the dead lying in the earth, before returning to the profane world. Neither the conversations nor the silence would be the same as one generally experiences after a performance at some Parisian theatre.

Death would be both closer and lighter, the theatre more solemn. There are other reasons. They are more subtle. It is up to you to discover them within yourselves without defining or naming them.

THE STRANGE WORD 'URB...'

☐ The monumental theatre – whose style remains yet to be discovered – ought to be as important as the Law Courts, as the monument to the war dead, the cathedral, the Houses of Parliament, the military academies, the seat of government, the clandestine place where black market goods and drugs are bought and sold, as the Observatory – and its function is to be all these things at once, but in a certain way: in a cemetery, or close by a crematorium oven, with its stiff, oblique, and phallic chimney.

☐ I'm not talking about a dead cemetery, but about a living one, that is, not one in which only a few steles remain standing. I'm talking about a cemetery in which graves are still being dug and the dead are being buried, I'm talking about a Crematorium where, day and night, corpses are being cooked.

☐ Page 4* will give you some idea, however vague and imperfect, of how I envisage a new theatre. When I speak of a favoured public, I am referring to certain persons with enough experience to comment upon the theatre in general, and upon the play being performed that day.

☐ Not having given a great deal of thought to the theatre, I still have the feeling that what matters is not to multiply the number of performances so that the greatest number of spectators can profit (?) from them, but rather to work so that the attempts – which are called rehearsals – culminate in one performance of such great intensity and brilliance that, by the spark it will have ignited in each spectator, it will suffice to

* This page no longer exists.

THE STRANGE WORD 'URB...'

illuminate those who did not take part in it, and make them uneasy.

☐ As for the audience, only those who know themselves capable of taking a nocturnal stroll through a cemetery, in order to be confronted with a mystery, will come to the theatre.
   If such an arrangement were made, deriving as much from urbanism as from culture, authors would be less frivolous, they would think twice before allowing their plays to be staged. Perhaps they would accept the marks of madness upon them, or the ranks of a frivolity approaching madness.

☐ With a kind of easy grace, cemeteries, after a certain length of time, allow themselves to be dispossessed. When no more burials take place cemeteries die, but in an elegant manner: lichen, saltpetre, moss cover the flagstones. A theatre built in a cemetery will perhaps die – it will be extinguished – like the cemetery itself. Will it perhaps disappear? It's possible that the theatrical art will disappear one day. That's a notion you have to accept. If someday man's activities were to become revolutionary, day after day, the theatre would have no place in life. Or if a dulling of the mind were to someday lead man to daydreaming, then the theatre would also die.

☐ To search for the origins of the theatre in History, and the origin of History in time, is stupid. A waste of time.
   What would we lose if we were to lose the theatre?

THE STRANGE WORD 'URB...'

☐ What will the cemeteries be like? An oven capable of decomposing the dead. If I speak of a theatre amongst the graves, it is because today the word 'death' is dark and mysterious, and in a world which seems to be moving so merrily towards analytical clarity, with nothing left with which to protect our translucent eye, like Mallarmé, I think we must add a bit of shadow. The various branches of science decipher everything, or try to, but we're at the end of our rope! We have to seek refuge elsewhere than within our ingeniously lighted entrails. . . . No, I'm mistaken: not seek refuge, but discover a new and torrid shadow, which will be our work.

☐ Even if the graves have become blurred, the cemetery will be well cared for, the Crematorium too. During the day, happy crews – there are some in Germany – will clean them while they whistle, and whistle in tune. The inside of the oven and chimney can remain black with soot.

☐ Where did I read that Rome – but my memory may be faulty – used to have a funeral mime? His role? To lead the funeral procession and mime the most important acts of the dead man's life.

To improvise gestures, attitudes?

Words. Having survived God knows how, the French language conceals and reveals a war of words, brotherly enemies, one snatching from the other or else falling in love with it. If tradition and treason are both born of the same original movement and diverge so that each can live its own particular life, how throughout the length and breadth of the language, do they know they are bound together in their distortion?

THE STRANGE WORD 'URB...'

No worse in this respect than any other language, but like the others French allows words to straddle each other like animals in heat, and what emerges from our mouths is an orgy of words which mate, innocently or not, and lend to French speech the wholesome appearance of a wooded countryside where all the stray animals flock together. Writing in such a language – or speaking it – one says nothing. All you do is allow a downpour of beings to swarm all the more in the midst of some idle vegetation of pollen, its haphazard graftings, its slips and suckers a welter of beings which swarms and embroils or, if you like, equivocal words, like the animals in the Fable.

If anyone is under the illusion that in the midst of proliferation – or luxuriance – of monsters he can hope to make any sense out of what he says, he is mistaken: at most, he can couple larval and crafty herds similar to the processions of processionary caterpillars, who will exchange their sperm in order to give birth to such a carnivalesque brood, as unimportant as it is inconsequential, descended from the Greek, the Anglo-Saxon, the Levantine, the Arab, the Latin, the Gaelic, from some stray Chinese, three strange Mongolian vagabonds who talk but say nothing but who, by mating, reveal a verbal orgy the meaning of which is lost not in the dark night of time but in an infinity of tender and brutal mutations.

And the funeral mime?

And the Theatre in the cemetery?

Before the dead man is buried, let him be borne in his casket to the front of the stage; let his friends, his enemies, and the merely curious gather in that part of the theatre normally reserved for the public; let the funeral mime who led the procession divide and multiply into two, into several groups; let him become a theatrical troupe; let him, in the presence of the dead and the public, recreate the life and death of the

THE STRANGE WORD 'URB...'

deceased; after that, in the dead of night, let the casket be borne to the grave; and finally let the public depart, the spectacle is over. Until a new ceremony, suggested by another dead man whose life is deemed worthy of a dramatic performance – not a tragic one. Tragedy has to be lived, not played.

If we are clever enough, we can pretend to understand, we can make believe that words are stable, that their meaning is fixed or that it has changed because of us who, voluntarily, people seem to believe, if we modify their appearance slightly, become gods. As for me, faced with this enraged herd encaged in the dictionary, I know that I have said nothing and that I never will: and the words don't give a damn.

Actions are hardly any more docile. As for language, there is a grammar of action: beware of the self-taught man!

Treason is perhaps part of tradition, but treason is in no way repose. I had to make a real effort to betray my friends: there was reward awaiting me when I did.

Therefore, for the main parade before the burial of the body, the funeral mime, if he wants to make the dead live and die again, will have to discover, and dare to say, those dialectophagous words which, in the presence of the public, will devour the life and the death of the dead man.

*What remained of a Rembrandt
torn up into very even
little pieces and chucked
into the crapper*

It is only that kind of truths – the truths that cannot be proven and that, in fact, are 'false', those that one cannot, without seeming absurd, carry to their ultimate conclusions without arriving at the negation both of the truths themselves and of oneself – these are the truths that ought to be exalted by any work of art. They will never have the good fortune – or the misfortune – to be one day applied. May they live by the song that they have become and that they inspire.

Something that reminded me of a putrescence was in the process of corrupting, like gangrene, the whole spectrum of my former vision of the world. When one day, in the compartment of some train, as I was looking at the passenger sitting across from me, I was suddenly

Our gaze can be sharp or dull, depending upon the object seen as much as, or more than, upon ourselves. That is why I speak of this speed, for example, that propels the object ahead of us, or of a slowness that makes it heavy.

When our eye fixes upon a Rembrandt painting (the later works) it becomes heavy, slightly bovine. Something – some solemn force – retains it. Why do we keep on looking, since we're not initially delighted by the intellectual liveliness which is all-encompassing and immediate – of a Guardi arabesque, for example?

Like a stable smell: when

struck by the realisation that any man *is worth* any other, I did not suspect – or rather I did, I vaguely did, for all at once I was overwhelmed by a wave of sadness, a wave which, although it was more or less bearable, remained with me ever after – I did not suspect that this realisation would result in such a methodical disintegration. Behind what was visible of this man, or farther – farther and at the same time miraculously and devastatingly near – in that man – face and body without charm, ugly; to judge by certain details, even vile: a foul moustache, which in itself is hardly worth complaining about, but it was hard, stiff, a moustache whose wings stuck out almost horizontally directly above his tiny mouth, his rotten mouth, from which he kept sending gobs of spit between his knees onto the floor of a car already soiled by a collection of cigarette butts, paper, bits and pieces of bread – in short, whatever it was in those days that constituted the filth of a third-class compartment – in that man's look I discovered, and was shocked by the discovery, a kind of identity common to all men.

all I see is the subject's torso (Hendrijke in Berlin) or only its head, I can't help imagining it standing on a pile of dung. Its lungs are breathing. Its hands are warm. Bony, gnarled, but warm. The table of the Cloth Merchant's official receiver is set on straw, the five men smell of cow piss and dung. Beneath Hendrijke's skirts, beneath the fur-trimmed greatcoats, beneath the dressing-gowns, beneath the painter's outlandish dress, the bodies are properly performing their functions: they are digesting, they are warm, they are heavy, they smell, they shit.

However finely chiselled her face and solemn her expression, The Jewish Fiancée *has an arse. You can smell it. She may at any moment lift her skirts. She may sit down, she has what it takes. Mrs. Trip does too. As for Rembrandt himself, it goes without saying: starting with his first portrait, his fleshly*

But hold on! All that did not take place in that order, or quite so quickly: first of all, my gaze struck head-on – not simply encountered – that of the traveller, or, rather, mine melted in his. The man in question had just raised his eyes from his newspaper and, very simply, and for no good reason, his eyes met mine, which just as accidentally happened to be looking at him.

Did he immediately experience the same emotion – and already the feeling of confusion – that I was experiencing? His gaze was not that of someone else: it was my own that I was meeting in a mirror, *inadvertently and in the solitude and the oblivion of myself*. What I was feeling at the time I can only translate in the following terms: I flowed out of my body, and through my eyes, into that of the traveller *at the same time as the traveller flowed into mine*. Or, rather, *I had flowed*, for the exchange of looks was so fast that I can only recall it with the help of that tense. The traveller had gone back to his reading. Utterly taken aback by what I had just discovered, I then, and only then, thought to examine the stranger, and the feeling of

mass will constantly increase from one painting to the next, until the very last, whither it arrives, definitive but not emptied of all substance. After he lost all he held most dear – his mother and his wife – it was as though this strapping fellow was bent on his own self-destruction, without regard for the people of Amsterdam, to vanish socially.

To wish to be nothing is an expression one often hears. It's a Christian thought: ought we to understand by it that man tries to lose, to allow to dissolve, what in one way or another distinguishes him in a commonplace manner, *what gives him his opacity, so that on the day of his death he can appear before God wholly transparent, not even iridescent? I don't know, and I couldn't care less.*

As for Rembrandt, his entire work leads me to

disgust I have already mentioned was the result of that examination: beneath his rumpled, seedy, colourless clothes his body was probably worn and dirty. His mouth was weak and protected by a poorly trimmed moustache, and I said to myself that in all likelihood this man was a spineless creature, probably a coward. He was more than fifty. The train continued on its way, moving indifferently from one French village to the next. It was coming up to dusk. The idea of spending these twilight moments, these moments of complicity, with this partner made me extremely uncomfortable.

What was it then that had flowed out of my body – I fl . . . – and what was it that flowed out of the body of my travelling companion?

This disagreeable experience, with its intensity or its sudden spontaneity, never happened to me again, but I was constantly aware of its repercussions from then on. What happened to me in that train compartment struck me as a kind of revelation: once you recognised and dismissed the accidents – which in this case were repulsive – of his

believe that he wasn't satisfied to rid himself of what encumbered him in order to accede to the transparency mentioned above; what he wanted was to transform it, modify it, make it serve the work. Rid the subject of its anecdotal qualities and place it beneath a light of eternity. Meaningful today, tomorrow, and for the dead. What would a work be offered to today's living, and the living of a future age, but not to the dead?

A Rembrandt painting not only stops the time which was making the subject flow towards the future, it also takes it back into the very depths of time. In so doing, Rembrandt summons solemnity. He therefore discovers why, at every moment, each event is solemn: for that, his own solitude teaches him.

But this quality of solemnity has to be transferred to the canvas, and it is here that appearance, this man concealed and then allowed me to discover what made him identical to me. (I first wrote that sentence, but then I corrected it with the following, which is both more precise and more distressing: I knew that I was identical to that man.)

Was it because any man is identical to any other?

While continuing to dwell on these thoughts throughout the remainder of the voyage, and with a kind of disgust with myself, I very quickly came to the conclusion that it was this identity that allowed any man to be loved – *neither any more nor any less* – just as much as any other, and that generalisation would have to include the most unspeakably foul or vile creatures. Nor did my thoughts stop at that. My ruminations also led me to this further notion: this appearance, which I had first labelled vile – the word is not too strong – was willed by this identity (that word stubbornly intruded again and again, but perhaps because at that time I did not yet possess a very rich vocabulary) which continued to make its way among all men and was revealed by a simple, unres-

his taste for theatricality – so keen when he was twenty-five – will serve him in good stead. It is possible that his immense sorrow – the death of Saskia – turned Rembrandt away from all the daily joys and pleasures, and that he gave expression to his mourning through the metamorphosis of golden chains, plumed hats, prominent swords, or rather in pictorial revelries. I don't know whether he cried, this Dutchman, but in the vicinity of his forty-second year he underwent a baptism by fire which, little by little, transformed his basic nature, vain and bold.

Because at twenty the strapping young fellow seems like a pretty tough customer, spending a fair share of his time in front of the mirror. He is conceited, thinks the world of himself, so young and already in the mirror! Not in order to slick himself up and run off to the ball, but to contemplate trained look. I even suspected that this appearance was the temporary form of the identity of all men. But this pure and virtually lifeless look that went from one to the other of the two travellers, this look in which conscious will played no part and which, had it been conscious, could probably have been prevented, lasted for only a brief moment, but that was enough for me to be flooded by a feeling of profound sadness, which remained with me from then on. I lived for a fairly long time with that discovery, which I purposely chose to keep to myself and the memory of which I constantly tried to put from my mind; but always, somewhere within me, there lurked a stain of sadness which suddenly, as though some breath had blown it up, darkened everything.

'It has been revealed to me,' I would say to myself, 'that every man, behind his charming or perhaps, to our eyes, monstrous appearance, retains a quality that seems to be like some final refuge, with the result that, in some very secret, and perhaps irreducible, realm he is what every other man is.'

himself at length, smugly, all by himself: Rembrandt with three moustaches, with furrowed brow, with unkempt hair, with circles under his eyes, etc. No deep concern is visible in this simulated search for identity. If he paints architectural works, they are always stage-set architecture. Then, little by little, without losing either his narcissism or his flair for the theatrical, he is going to change them: the former to arrive at anxiety, to the wildness that he will come to transcend, the latter to derive joys – also haggard – from the slave of the 'Jewish Fiancée'.

With Saskia's death – I wonder whether he didn't kill her in one way or another, whether he wasn't delighted by her death – his hand and eye are free. From then on he undertakes a kind of extravagance in painting: with Saskia dead, the world and social judgments are of

I even thought I found that equivalence at the Halles in Paris, in the slaughter-houses in the staring but not expressionless eyes of the bodyless heads of sheep, stacked in pyramids on the counter. Where would I stop? Who might I have murdered if I had killed some leopard whose long strides were like the hooligans of yesteryear?

You may remember that I had mentioned earlier that my dearest friends took refuge, I was quite certain, in some secret wound. Or, rather, I wrote: '. . . in some very secret, and perhaps irreducible, realm . . .' Was I speaking of the same thing? One man was the same as any other: that was the truth that had jarred me like a slap. But was it really so rare to learn such a truth that I was filled with wonder at the revelation? And, once I had learned it, how could it contribute to my self-advancement? First, it is one thing to learn something through a process of analysis, and quite another to seize it through some sudden intuition. (For it goes without saying that I had often heard, or read, that all men are equal, and even that all men are brothers.) But progress

little importance. You have to picture him, with Saskia dying and he perched on his ladders in his studio, regrouping the arrangement of the Nightwatch. *Does he believe in God? Not when he paints. He knows his Bible and makes good use of it.*

It goes without saying that what I have just said is important only insofar as one accepts that everything was virtually false. A work of art, if it is finished, cannot be used as the basis for insights and intellectual games. It would even seem to confuse the mind, or bind it. Well, I played.

In a certain way, works of art would make us assinine if their fascination was not the proof – uncontrollable and yet indisputable – that this paralysis of the intellect intermingles with and is identical to the most luminous certainty. Which, I find impossible to say. The towards what? One thing was more certain: it was impossible not to have learned what I had learned on the train.

How had I passed from the knowledge that every man resembles any other to the notion that every man *is* every other man, I was incapable of saying. But the idea was implanted in me. It was in me like a conviction. More clearly – but then I am going to deflower it slightly – it might be expressed by the following aphorism: 'There exists, and has always existed, but one single man in the world. He is completely in each of us, therefore he is we. Each man is the other and the others. In the relaxed atmosphere of evening, a limpid look exchanged – cast or barely darted, I was ignorant of the technique – made us aware of it. With the exception that one phenomenon, whose name I do not even know, seems to divide this unique man infinitely, apparently fragments him in accident and in form, and makes each of the fragments unfamiliar to us.'

I went from one weighty explanation to another, and what I felt was even more chaotic and

source for these lines is my feeling (in London, twelve years ago) when confronted with his most beautiful paintings. What then is the matter with me? Why this reaction? What are these paintings I have such difficulty extricating from me? Who is this Mrs. Trip? That gentleman? . . .

No. I have never wondered who these ladies and gentlemen were. And perhaps, more or less cleanly, it is this lack of any question that makes me twitch? The more I looked at them, the less these portraits reminded me of people I knew. Of no one. It probably took me a long time to arrive at this heart-breaking and intoxicating idea: the portraits Rembrandt painted (after his fiftieth year) relate to no known person. No detail, no facial feature, refers to any character trait, any particular psychology. Are they depersonalised by some diagrammatic method?

stronger than the idea I have already spoken of and which, rather than thought, was dreamt, engendered, dragged or dredged up by some rather lifeless dream.

No man was my brother: every man was me, but isolated, temporarily, in his own very special skin. The fact is, that realisation did not lead me to examine, or re-examine, the whole system of moral values. With respect to this 'me' outside of my own particular appearance, I felt no tenderness, no affection. Nor with respect to that form assumed by the other – or his prison. Or his grave? On the contrary, I had a tendency to be as tough, as uncompromising, with it as I was with that shape which answered to my name and penned these lines. What bothered me the most was that sadness with which I had been overwhelmed. Since I had experienced that revelation by looking at that traveller on the train, it had been impossible for me to view the world as I had formerly done. Nothing was certain or solid. Suddenly the world was a floating world. For a long time I remained sickened and disgusted by my discovery, but I had a premonition

Not at all. One has only to think of Margaretha Trip's wrinkles. And the more I looked, hoping to seize, or approach, the personality, as the expression has it, to discover their particular identity, the more they slipped away – without exception – into an infinite flight, all at the same speed. Only Rembrandt himself – perhaps because of the acuity of his gaze contemplating his own image – retained some modicum of his individuality: at least the attention. But the others, if I counted this profound sadness as trifling, slipped away without allowing anything to be seized.

Trifling, that sadness? That of another world? Nothing else than the attitude naturally assumed by people when they are alone, waiting to act in this or that manner. He, Rembrandt, in his portrait at Cologne, in which he is laughing. The face and background are

that within a very short period of time I would be compelled to make some serious changes, which I rather suspected would be renunciations. My sadness was an indication. It had, in a third-class train car, between Salon and Saint-Rambert-d'Albon, just lost its beautiful colours, its charms. I was already bidding them a fond farewell, and it was with a feeling of both sadness and disgust that I set forth along those paths that were always bound to be more solitary, and especially among those visions of the world which, instead of intensifying my joy, only made me all the more disgusted.

'At the rate things are going,' I told myself, 'it will not be long before all the things I used to cherish will be worthless: loves, friendship, formalities, vanity – whatever stems from seduction.'

But perhaps this look – this atrociously revealing look – which had chanced to light on the traveller was made possible because of a basic bent of my character, or because of my life, or because of some other reason. I was not at all convinced that another man would have been able to feel himself flow,

so red that the whole painting makes one think of a placenta dried in the sun.

In the Cologne museum, there is not much room to step back away from the paintings. You have to look at them at an angle, diagonally. It was from this angle that I looked at them, head down – my head – upside-down as it were. Blood rushed to my head, but how sad was this laughing face!

It is from the time when he depersonalises his models, when he removes all identifiable characteristics from the objects, that he gives to both their greatest reality, makes them most convincing.

Something important happened: at the same time as the eye recognises the object, it recognises painting for what it is. And he will never deviate from it. Rembrandt does not distort through his look, into someone else's body, nor that the meaning he might lend to the feeling would be the same as the one I'm offering here. Always tempted to doubt and question the established values of the world in which I lived, perhaps I was once again trying to slip myself into individual envelopes the better to deny the notion of singularity?

'It will not be long before nothing will matter any more. . . .' Or that nothing would be changed? If every envelope preciously conceals a same identity then every envelope is singular and succeeds in establishing between us an opposition which seems irremediable, in creating an infinite variety of individuals who are equal: one = the other. Perhaps the only particularity of every man, the only things real and precious about him were: 'his' moustaches, 'his' eyes, 'his' clubfoot, 'his' harelip. And what if he had, as a source of self-pride, nothing but the dimensions of 'his' pedukah? But this look went from the unknown traveller to me, and in a flash I knew for certain that the one-the other was one and the same, at once either me or him, and me

painting by trying to blend it into the object or the face it is commissioned to portray: he offers it to us as a distinct and separate material, which is unashamed to be what it is. The candour of the fields plowed in the morning, smoking. I'm not sure what the viewer gains, but the painter gains the candour of his profession. He portrays himself in his madness as a dauber crazy about colour, losing the feigned superiority and the hypocrisy of his imitators. This will be most evident in his late paintings. But it was necessary for Rembrandt to recognise himself for what he was and to accept himself as a flesh-and-blood person – what am I saying, flesh-and-blood? – a person of meat, cheap meat, of blood, sweat tears, shit, of intelligence and tenderness, and of other things too ad infinitum, none of which cancelled out the others. Better: all of which greeted the others respectfully.

and him. And how could one forget that phlegm?

Let's go on. Knowing what I had just learned, it was not a question of bending my efforts towards keeping with the dictates of the revelation in order to lose myself in some ill-defined contemplation. It was simply that henceforth I could no longer pretend *not* to know what I knew, and I had to pursue the consequences whatever they turned out to be. Since various incidents in my life had turned me to poetry, perhaps the poet ought to feel compelled to utilise this new discovery in some way. But I must first and foremost make the following observation: the only moments in my life that I hold to be true, stripping away my exterior and revealing in all its nakedness . . . what? *a solid void* which enabled me to go on living? – I believe I can say that I experienced them in the course of several unholy fits of anger, at times when I was prey to some ungodly fear, and in the ray – the first – which passed between a young man's eye and my own, in that initial look exchanged between us. And, too, in that look that went from the

And it goes without saying that all of Rembrandt's work is only meaningful – at least to me – if I know that what I have just written is false.

traveller to me. The rest, all the rest, struck me as being the effect of some optical error caused by my appearance, which in itself was of necessity faked. Rembrandt was the first to denounce me. Rembrandt! That serious finger which pulls aside the cheap finery to reveal... what? An infinitude, an infernal transparency.

So I was feeling profoundly disgusted for what I was moving towards, something I did not understand but, thank God, could not avoid, and I was also feeling very sad about what I was about to lose of myself. All my illusions began to wither away, everything grew stale and rotten. Eroticism and its attendant furies seemed denied me, once and for all. How could I remain unaware of the fact that, after the experience in the train compartment, any charming shape or form, even though it contains me, is me? Which meant that, if I wanted to recapture that identity, any form, be it pleasant or frightful, would lose its power over me.

'The erotic quest', I would say to myself, 'is possible only when one recognises the individuality of every being, when that individuality is irreducible and the physical form attests to it and only it.'

What did I know about the sense or substance of the erotic? But the notion that I was going around in every man, that every man was me filled me with disgust. If for a period of time any rather handsome – and male – human form (and I'm referring to the conventional sense of handsome) maintained a certain sway over me, one could explain it as being a kind of reverberation. This power was the reflection of the power to which I had yielded for so long a time. A nostalgic greeting to that power, too. Thus no one any longer appeared to me in his complete, his absolute, his magnificent individuality: a fragmentary appearance of a single being, it disgusted me even more. And yet as I wrote what you have just read I continued to be concerned, tormented, by the erotic themes which were familiar to me and had dominated my life. I was sincere when I spoke about a quest stemming from the revelation that 'any man is every other man, and that includes me', but I also knew I was writing that in an effort to rid myself of eroticism, to dislodge it, or at least create a distance between it and me. An erect member, throbbing and gorged with blood, standing in a thicket of black, curly hair, and then that which forms the continuation thereof: the sturdy thighs, then the torso, the entire body, the hands, the thumbs, then the neck, the lips, the nose, the hair, and last but not least the eyes which summon the amatory furies as though to be rescued or annihilated, all of which was fighting tooth and nail against the look, the look so fragile and yet perhaps capable of destroying that Almighty.